T0128156

WWII ESSAYS

WWII ESSAYS

A COMPENDIUM OF WAR LORE

WILLIAM T. BERAN

iUniverse®

WWII ESSAYS
A COMPENDIUM OF WAR LORE

iUniverse books may be ordered through booksellers or by contacting:

iUniverse
1663 Liberty Drive
Bloomington, IN 47403
www.iuniverse.com
1-800-Authors (1-800-288-4677)

Because of the dynamic nature of the Internet, any web addresses or links contained in this book may have changed since publication and may no longer be valid. The views expressed in this work are solely those of the author and do not necessarily reflect the views of the publisher, and the publisher hereby disclaims any responsibility for them.

Any people depicted in stock imagery provided by Thinkstock are models, and such images are being used for illustrative purposes only. Certain stock imagery © Thinkstock.

ISBN: 978-1-5320-1343-0 (sc)
ISBN: 978-1-5320-1344-7 (e)

Library of Congress Control Number: 2016921079

Print information available on the last page.

iUniverse rev. date: 01/10/2017

CONTENTS

INTRODUCTION

World War II is engrained in the memories of millions, especially those of us who experienced it firsthand. From the home front to the front lines, the war occupied everyone's life and lifestyle. We at home followed the war reports nonstop via radio, magazines, and newspapers. In fact, the media was so saturated with war news that I, a ten-year old by V-J Day, couldn't imagine what would be talked about *after* the war. Mother assured me they'd find other things to report.

Most of the movies and news reels made during the war naturally portrayed the conflict in terms that were clearly partial to the Allies. They usually depicted us facing our sacrifices and commitments with implacable resolve and courage, whether on the battlefield or on the home front. This strong patriotic spin abated rather quickly after the war, although it was somewhat revitalized later with the onset of the Cold War and the Korean "Police Action."

For years afterward, World War II stories carried by radio, TV, movies, and books were very popular. Some very good documentaries (for example, TV's 1952 *Victory at Sea*) and melodramas (for example, Hollywood's 1946 *The Best Years of Our Lives*) were produced.

Unadorned documentaries could probably keep hard-core historians and military enthusiasts engrossed, but more sentimentality (human interest content) was generally needed to consistently grab the general public's attention. Broader public interest was also engaged by employing exposé themes, such as stories that unearthed military secrets, aired moral dilemmas, or revealed shocking new discoveries of wartime events.

War stories from an enemy citizen's or soldier's point of view eventually emerged, often depicting the enemy's own victimization or heroics during the war (for example, the early-eighties acclaimed *Das Boot*). These often impressed the viewer as being a particularly evenhanded and accurate rendering of events, and evoked some sympathy, because they usually depicted our former enemies' tragic endings.

My own thoughts on selected events of that era are found in the following essays. Included are condensed facts regarding the war, some of the prevailing "mood du jour" and a smattering of (what I deem) unpretentious personal insight. A few of these essays are clearly autobiographical. Even if you're not a World War II buff, I hope you find these essays engagingly informative.

European Leaders at 1938 Munich Peace
Conference (Chamberlain at left)

Chamberlain—Prudent Appeasement

In 1938, British Prime Minister Neville Chamberlain was highly criticized by Winston Churchill and others for his "appeasement policy" regarding Nazi Germany's threatened annexation of the Sudetenland, a border area of northern Czechoslovakia mostly inhabited by ethnic Germans. The truth was that Britain lacked the military might to meaningfully challenge the hostilities then threatening them by Japan (in Asia), Germany (in Europe), and Italy (the Mediterranean and Africa). Their major European allies at the time (France and Poland) were also ill-prepared for a war with Nazi Germany, and the United States was staunchly neutral. It was clear that little military assistance would be forthcoming from Britain's allies to confront the Nazis. Throwing down the gauntlet to resolve the Sudetenland issue could've been seen as morally legitimate, but likely would have led to militarily disaster.

Instead, Chamberlain, along with representatives from France and Italy, signed the Munich Agreement with Hitler in September 1938. It permitted Germany a peaceful annexation of the Sudetenland. As Hitler had earlier threatened to return that area to Germany by force, Chamberlain announced to a relieved Britain that the Munich Agreement brought "peace for our time." The "our time" part lasted for about a year, a period during which Chamberlain's critics felt vindicated when Hitler's territorial appetite became clearly evident.

Although the appeasement policy had failed per se, it gave Britain valuable time to build Spitfire and Hurricane fighters as well as acquire airfields, pilots, and ground crews needed to win the Battle of Britain. It also allowed time for Britain to fine-tune their air raid early-warning tactics, particularly the Filter Room at Bentley Priory that integrated the information from Chain Home radar stations, Home Guard Spotters, and signal intelligence into a remarkably efficient air defense system.

The Munich Agreement was Chamberlain's pragmatic alternative to the folly of entering a war when military resources to wage a successful campaign were unavailable. Chamberlain was neither timid nor naive, as his political critics intimated. In fact, he had motivated Britain to begin war preparations a full two years before the Munich Agreement was signed. He also had consummated military alliances (weak as they were) to discourage Nazi expansionism. But without the Munich Agreement, Britain may have faced the Luftwaffe onslaught in 1938 instead of 1940, and Germany would then have more likely gained the air superiority it needed to open the door for a successful invasion of the British Isles.

Japanese Battle Flag

Japan—No Holds Barred, No Quarter Given

The Pearl Harbor attack on December 7, 1941, the "date which will live in infamy," as President Roosevelt put it, is regarded as the defining event that catapulted the United States formally into World War II. However, the root cause of this attack goes back years earlier (1937) to the reprehensible Rape of Nanking by the invading Japanese troops in China. This unspeakable treatment of civilian men, women, and children, combined with subsequent Japanese atrocities and intentions to occupy French Indo-China, motivated the United States to threaten withholding its metal and oil exports to Japan unless they relinquished their occupied Asian territories.

Japan's purpose for invading China in the first place was to gain direct control of many natural resources their island nation sorely needed. Therefore, abandoning these hard-won resources—and losing face in the process—wasn't an option Japan could stomach. Now faced with a full-blown US oil embargo (we supplied 80 percent of their oil) and cancellation of oil contracts by the Dutch East Indies (who supplied virtually all the rest), Japan determined that they quickly needed to take over the Southeast Asia oil fields by force, before their rapidly dwindling oil reserves would run out and render them powerless.

Japan's new invasions could be successfully implemented only by first crippling their biggest obstacle, the American Pacific fleet at Pearl Harbor. If that was done, Japan reasoned it could fight off the anticipated United States, British, and Australian counterattacks by virtue of their superior naval force and their army's perceived invincibility. Their objective was to at least force a stalemate in the ensuing military engagements, leaving the captured oil fields and other strategic resources under Japanese control with or without a peace treaty.

This strategy was implemented, as we rudely found out, when Japan launched their large-scale preemptive aircraft strike at Pearl Harbor and gained an unforgettable tactical victory. Simultaneously, their invasions of Southeast Asia's islands and countries, as well as the Philippine Islands and Wake Island, stunned the Allies. Japan had them clearly out-maneuvered and out-gunned.

Japan's strategy worked as planned until the Battle of Midway, June 1942. The incredible American victory during that historic naval engagement forecast the ultimate unraveling of Japan's grand plan. With the enormous losses sustained by the Imperial Navy over the course of just a few hours, a successful military stalemate in the Pacific theater suddenly became problematic.

Manzanar—One of Ten World
War II Relocation Centers

3

Internment—Guilt by Racial Association

The wartime policy of interning Japanese Americans in "relocation centers" after the Pearl Harbor attack was regarded years later as grossly unfair, a violation of civil rights, sanctioned theft of private property, and motivated by racial discrimination. In 1988, a presidential apology was offered, with legislation citing "race prejudice, war hysteria, and a failure of political leadership" for the actions.

Subsequently, reparations of over $1.6 billion were paid to those interned for the injustice. This purging of American guilt was not similarly extended to German Americans or Italian Americans, some of whom were also interned. They were much fewer in number than Japanese Americans, but their confinement was equally unjustified in most cases.

Because the Japanese Americans were racially identified with a nation that apparently sanctioned horrific atrocities, there was generally more fear, distrust, and racial bias toward them than toward the other two nationalities. The successful Japanese attack on Pearl Harbor revived images of their Rape of Nanking and other outrages. It also reinforced their image as masters of treachery, given that the United States and Japan were engaged in peace negotiations at the time. The bizarre Niihau Incident that followed the Pearl Harbor attack also convinced US authorities that previously loyal Japanese Americans could be persuaded or intimidated into switching allegiance.

The December 7 attack made it abundantly clear that "their" nation was now coming after us. Preparations for a possible Japanese invasion of our mainland included delineating an "exclusion zone" for all Japanese aliens and Japanese Americans within one hundred miles of the West Coast (Canada quickly followed suit). This removed them physically from the anticipated combat zone, obviously neutralizing their perceived security risk, but also eliminating any opportunity for "mistakes" by the Caucasian defenders. Particularly then, many Americans felt "the only good Jap was a dead Jap." With Japanese Americans in guarded internment camps away from public access, some were probably saved from outright criminal injury or death, given the country's ramped-up contempt for anything Japanese.

This nationwide antipathy toward Japanese Americans (some might call it a pack mentality) was a predictable response to a perceived threat from an extremely barbaric adversary. Such behavior was not solely consigned to a mid-twentieth century mindset, nor to only Americans. As recent events exemplify, animosity is easily aroused and misplaced when racial, religious, or cultural characteristics of innocent bystanders resemble that of one's foe; it's as if they're wearing the enemy uniform.

U-Boat Cutaway

U-Boat War—Human and Environmental Disaster of the First Order

Over twelve million tons of US merchant shipping was sunk by U-boats during the war. Most vessels were blown apart by torpedoes, mines, or deck guns, and thus spewed their contents freely into the sea. Those contents consisted of cargo (munitions, armament, raw petroleum, refined petroleum, food, clothing, troops), the ships' food and fuel (Bunker C, diesel), and crew members.

Over the course of the war, nearly ten thousand Merchant Marines lost their lives this way. This was stoically endured without a lot of publicity in order to conceal from the enemy the stunning loses inflicted by the U-boat campaign. Reporting actual losses likely would also have stifled recruiting efforts and dampened national morale. The Merchant Marines proportionately suffered far more combat deaths than any other branch of military service during the war.

The collateral environmental impact and loss of ocean life is difficult to ascertain, but given the amount of explosives detonated to inflict the massive shipping losses, the effect must have been huge; probably many hundred million food fish were destroyed along with tons of other marine flora and fauna. On top of that, still more explosives were used by the Allies in the bombing and depth-charge counterattacks attempting to sink the U-boats.

The older U-boats contained hundreds of pounds of mercury in internal piping systems to shift weight fore and aft to trim the submarine when submerged (later U-boats and those of other nations used water for that purpose). When sunk, those U-boats immediately or eventually leaked a large amount of this enduringly toxic material into the marine environment. One sunken U-boat off the coast of Norway also happened to be carrying a cargo of seventy tons of mercury.

Among the U-boats' successful attacks were about four hundred merchant ships sunk just off the US East Coast and near shore in the Gulf of Mexico. This resulted in dead sailors, dead fish, miles of oil slicks, and tons of debris washing ashore. Tar balls were as common as seashells on some beaches. Cleanup work was not for the fainthearted, and a day at the beach during wartime took on new meaning.

Ironically, most of the sunken wreckage eventually evolved into artificial reefs that are veritable havens for sea life. But the hard truth is, some of this sea life is still chemically contaminated and unfit for human consumption.

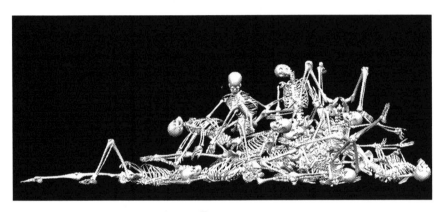

Bones

Holocaust—Beyond the Six Million

Hitler's personal disdain of Jews and his contrivance to use them as scapegoats for Germany's economic woes were lead-ins to what became the infamous genocide known as the Holocaust. His ultimate goal was to purge the Third Reich of "inferior" humans and, while at it, pilfer the wealth of those innocent victims. (Reportedly many billions of Jewish Reichsmarks were confiscated, which financed a sizable portion of the Nazi war machine.) As history shows, genocide was not invented by Hitler, but the scope of the Nazi's "Final Solution" for those of Jewish descent was unprecedented: an estimated six million were systematically murdered, wiping out about two thirds of the Jewish population in Europe.

As repugnant as this was, the Nazis even topped that by eventually killing more than ten million Slavs, almost two million ethnic Poles, a million or more Romani (Gypsies), and tens of thousands of handicapped people, political dissenters, Freemasons, Slovenes, and homosexuals. Even thousands of Jehovah's Witnesses were killed because, in staying true to their religious tenets, they rejected an oath of Nazi loyalty.

Italian fascists also had a share of blood on their hands. They operated deplorable concentration camps, mercilessly slaughtered civilians, and, in Ethiopia, used poison gas against enemy troops and even Red Cross personnel. However, after their surrender to the Allies in 1943, the Italians' culpability was suppressed as a quid pro quo for their support in aiding the Allies to drive the Nazis out of Italy, for their immediate declaration of war on Japan, and for their apparent political aversion to communism. After the war, historical revisionism took hold, and Italy was reinvented as a victim of Nazi tyranny and Balkan retribution.

The Japanese army's penchant for torture and murder of noncombatants, as well as enemy combatants, was exposed well before World War II started. Japan's culture had embraced a bastardized Bushido code that was Machiavellian to the core. As in the Nazi ideology, victims were regarded as weak, contemptible subhumans, and action taken to terminate these lives was regarded as a service to their society. Over fifteen million Chinese civilians paid the ultimate price for Japan's incursions into their country before and during World War II.

Looking back at these murderous doctrines and the merciless persistence in carrying them out reminds us that the layer of moral decency to which we civilized humans like to lay claim is, in actuality, a vulnerable thin veneer.

Stomping on a Tin Can

6

Tin Cans—The Flattened Reserves

Recycling, electric power conservation, food rationing, Red Cross first-aid courses, air raid drills, and blackout exercises were regular routines during World War II. Automobile production had ceased because aircraft, tanks, jeeps, cannon, and other war materials took over the production lines. A speed limit of 35 mph was imposed nationwide to conserve gasoline (which was also rationed) and preserve tires (only retreads and inner tube patches kept civilians going). Daylight savings time was restarted.

High schools and colleges changed curriculum to jumpstart training for war. My dad, who was not drafted into the armed service because of his "critical occupation" status as a high school teacher, took a crash course in summer of 1942 to learn and then teach aeronautics to his male students. Airplane identification skills were also honed, usually with simple three-view black silhouettes. To this day, I have an old deck of playing cards depicting an Allied or Axis airplane this way on each of the fifty-two cards.

Civilians regularly participated in scrap drives. This meant relinquishing or scrounging strategic materials and carting them off to a pickup point. Such materials included paper, rubber, lead, tin, iron, copper, brass, and aluminum. We also saved cooking grease (for glycerin, used in making explosives) and collected milkweed pods (for their fluffy seeds, used in aviators' flotation vests).

The most tedious job I had was flattening used tin cans. The standardized drill was to clean out any residue, strip off the label, cut out both ends of the can, and put them inside the can before smashing it flat. Bushel baskets full of these poured in from every household and town across the nation. The official reason for this initiative was that the cans were essential for extracting tin and steel.

Huge inventories of these flat cans piled up around the country because, unknown to the general public, technology was lacking then for efficiently separating and smelting the two metals. It was easier to keep using the current iron and tin ore sources as long as they held out, keeping the flattened cans as emergency reserve.

This technical problem was never officially divulged to the citizenry during or after the war. A possible motive for the lack of candor is that it might have undermined confidence and enthusiasm in this and other initiatives if it were found out the program was not quite implemented as advertised. After the war ended victoriously, it was more expedient to simply forget about the issue and silently write it off as one of war's little snafus— probably a justifiable recourse, since it hadn't cost lives.

President Roosevelt and Prime Minister Churchill
Casablanca Conference, 1943

Unconditional Surrender—
Surprise Attack by the Allies

The January 1943 Big Three Conference in Casablanca turned out to be a Big Two as a particularly nasty winter and the war crises in the Soviet Union forced its leader, Stalin, to stay home. This left the business of war strategy talks to US President Roosevelt and Britain Prime Minister Churchill.

Roosevelt announced his idea of unconditional surrender, almost (it would seem) as an afterthought. Churchill was apparently surprised by this idea but still maintained unqualified support of the policy in his public statements. Stalin was not initially enthused when informed of this policy decision. Unofficially, many leading generals, including Eisenhower, privately expressed concern that this policy would extend the war and add more casualties, since a negotiated peace was impossible.

Indeed, it would seem that Roosevelt's strategy was to fight to the finish in order to eliminate all political seeds of German Nazism, Italian fascism, and Japanese imperialism. It also blunted any intentions Stalin might have had to eventually negotiate a separate armistice with Hitler and thereby allow the Nazis to focus their war effort against only Britain and America.

The unconditional surrender terms made it clear that no harm was intended for the Axis general population following capitulation, but the military and political leaders would be held accountable for their actions prior to and during the conflict. The Nazi minister of propaganda, Joseph Goebbels, declared otherwise, inciting the German people to fight for their lives using the reasoning that defeat meant extinction of the German race.

Just how many additional war casualties this policy caused during the conflict is conjecture. Roosevelt and Churchill, particularly, loathed the thought of dealing with Axis tyrants under the auspices of a negotiated armistice. For one thing, there wouldn't be a truly recognized defeat of the enemy and their malevolent ideology; their eventual return to prewar strength could start the whole process over again, much as Germany had done after the World War I armistice. But just as important, war-crime perpetrators wouldn't face trial and punishment for their atrocities if the peace terms were negotiated with those very perpetrators.

Of course, we'll never know if this actually was the best strategy. But unconditional surrender combined with humane treatment of the former adversaries seems to have stabilized a torn-up postwar world and prevented a recurrence of the World War I fallout.

Atomic Bomb Explosion

8

The Bomb—Taming the Atom for Destruction

The US atomic bomb program, the Manhattan Project, mercifully outstripped Germany's for a number of reasons: (1) the high priority of and expenditure of money on the program ($26 billion in today's dollars); (2) the availability of very talented Jewish German physicists (mid-1930s refugees); (3) the destruction of deuterium (heavy water) supplies vitally needed by the German scientists' as their chosen neutron moderator; and (4) the German rocket program's higher priority (the V-1 and V-2 rocket developments were Germany's equivalent of our Manhattan Project).

The Manhattan Project entailed research programs not only in the United States, but in Canada and Britain as well. Despite thirty sites and 130,000 people working on the program, secrecy was maintained throughout the six-year development (except perhaps for Soviet spies). Not even Vice President Harry Truman knew about the effort until he became president upon Roosevelt's death in April 1945.

Another facet of the atomic bomb weapons package was the development of the B-29 bomber, needed to make the heavy deliveries to Japanese targets. This bomber pushed the state of technology, and its development costs exceeded that of even the Manhattan Project. The public was kept largely in the dark about its development, although rumors persisted about a Boeing super-bomber in the works. Combat operations with the B-29 began, and the secret was unveiled in mid-1944.

Firebombing of Japanese cities and dropping mines in shipping lanes and harbors by B-29s created immense destruction on land and sea in the year prior to the atomic bomb attacks. Unfortunately, this had little effect on the Japanese attitude regarding surrender. The Allies' Unconditional Surrender policy was probably *not* a factor; the Japanese culture with its engrained Bushido mentality forbid *any* kind of surrender by Japanese combatants. If Japan was invaded, anyone who could lift a bamboo spear would be a combatant and thus likely to fight to the death or, alternatively, commit suicide (as in Saipan).

However, after Hiroshima and Nagasaki, Emperor Hirohito saw that the Americans had both the means and the will to annihilate the Japanese, even without invading the home islands. Narrowly escaping a coup by military diehards, Hirohito finally announced Japan's surrender. "Unconditional" wasn't strictly enforced when the Allies wisely accepted Japanese terms to retain their emperor. But, in the end, World War II handed Japan its first defeat since AD 663.

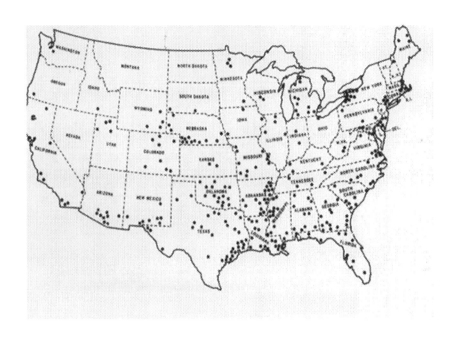

Map of Major WWII POW Camp Locations

(A Total of 500 Camps were Scattered Around the U.S.)

9

German POWs—Luxurious Internment

About four hundred thousand German prisoners of war (POWs) were eventually taken on by the United States at the request of Britain after the United States entered the war. Most were interned in military-style barrack compounds enclosed by barbed wire and watchtowers. To comply with the Geneva Convention, prisoners had decent quarters, clothing, food, military wages, recreational facilities, exposure to educational opportunities, and other amenities comparable to US Army standards. Because the war created a shortage of civilian manpower, some POWs were released to work in factories under armed guard. They even received added wages (about half the going union rate) for these efforts.

The factory of choice in my hometown was the local Stokely canning plant, where summer crops of peas and beans were processed. My dad's summer job was as a field agent who determined when and what fields would be cultivated, sprayed, and harvested. He occasionally took me along for a morning's workout in the fields, after which we wound up back at the plant where the POWs were laboring.

The POWs wore plain work uniforms with the initials P and W boldly emblazoned front and back on their shirts and pants.

Their demeanor generally wasn't hostile, although I still have an image of one glaring at me. The few guards had shotguns and .45 pistols, but they seemed to be terribly outnumbered. At any rate, no breakouts or serious acts of defiance ever materialized that I'm aware of. Besides, they had three good meals a day and break snacks in between, plenty of work to keep them occupied (a sixteen-hour workday seven days a week at the peak of the packing season), a nice bunkhouse, hot and cold running water, and dapper POW work clothes.

Given the relatively comfy lifestyle, the regular reindoctrination movies, and the Atlantic Ocean providing a huge barrier for return to combat duty in Germany, there was little incentive to escape. Only about half a percentage point of all prisoners made escape attempts, and with only a few exceptions, all escapees were caught sooner or later. Many escapees apparently regarded their actions as a diversion from prison camp life rather than expecting to reach Germany to fight anew.

Numerous German prisoners developed a rapport with the United States because of this extraordinarily humane treatment. Prisoners of war often acquired more money, food, and access to educational opportunities than they would have had back in Germany—more, for that matter, than was possible for many US citizens.

Homegrown Veggies

10

Victory Gardens—America's Urban Mini-farmers

With many hungry folks to feed in England and other foreign countries, and with cargo being regularly torpedoed in the Atlantic, the US food supplies were inevitably stretched to the limit. Food rationing was a necessary outcome of all the waste and extra mouths to feed.

On top of that, the internment of Japanese Americans on the West Coast after Pearl Harbor had a major unintended consequence: the sudden depletion of a large number of experienced fruit, nut, and vegetable farmers on California farms. About two hundred thousand acres were confiscated and transferred to migrating Dust Bowl farmers and other immigrants. These replacement farmers were unfamiliar with both the region and the crop, and they simply couldn't match the agricultural output of the displaced Japanese American farmers. This was a significant disruption that stimulated the government to launch still another strategy: a massive Victory Garden campaign.

Americans were asked to grow vegetables in their backyards, on penthouse rooftops, and on public lots. The federal Department of Agriculture and numerous popular magazines of the day gave helpful advice on making garden warriors out of people who had never grown plants or canned anything in their lives. By extolling patriotism as well as stressing the obvious practicalities (the harvest cost less and wasn't rationed), the effort became very successful. Nearly twenty million Americans took up the hoe and produced over a third of total US consumption of vegetables in 1943–45.

Gardening on public land, with other members of the community pitching in, turned out to be something of a social affair, although I do recall occasional conflicts of opinion about how the crops should be grown (akin with "too many cooks in the kitchen"). I also remember planting seeds and watering the garden with my mother, and the numerous trips back to the community site to look after the crops and ultimately harvest them for consumption or canning. In those days, you didn't have to be told to eat your veggies; there wasn't a lot of anything else around.

Despite the Victory Gardens being immensely successful, most folks dropped them like a hot potato when the war was over. Their obvious preference was to simply pop by the grocery store and pick food from neatly arranged bins. Now a major incentive to grow our own is the organic benefits (no chemical fertilizers, pesticides, and fungicides). However, this reason generally wasn't on the V-gardeners' radar.

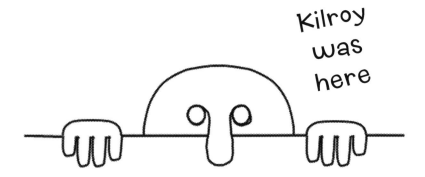

Kilroy
was
here

Kilroy Was Here, There, and Everywhere

The pictured graffiti could be found almost anywhere an American was located during the war years. It was one of those curious fads that pervade an entire society, but its roots are obscure. It had an unusually long period of popularity, beginning in the early 1940s and extending well into the 1950s.

Understandably, it being scribbled all over the place in public places was a bit tiresome, and many blatant examples were immediately rubbed out by the authorities. But the more "sophisticated" artists liked to create these whimsical masterpieces in hidden areas, to pop up at you without warning when you opened something, like a book, a drawer, a cupboard door, or a toilet seat.

Some very imaginative and patient artists even found the time to insert these figures in seemingly sealed articles, like a new deck of cards or a pack of cigarettes. Of course, this took far more skill than creating the drawing itself, so there was more to the game than displaying artistic mastery. Many more minutes (or hours) were spent dreaming up and implementing the gambit than were spent chuckling over it after the trap was sprung.

It's hard to fathom the enduring passion folks had for creating this stuff over and over. Some types of graffiti are a virtual work of art—Kilroy was anything but that. It was a simple and innocently absurd rendering created with the intention of surprising and amusing the "victim." Perhaps the commendable intention of creating some comic relief added to its staying power. Plus, as noted earlier, there was the abiding challenge of placing it in the most unlikely place imaginable in order to create the maximum benefit.

Comparable graffiti had apparently preceded Kilroy, both in Britain and Australia, but under different monikers. Similar doodles also originated in such diverse countries as Peru, Chile, Poland, and Russia. Like Kilroy, all were apparently done for the collective amusement of both donor and recipient.

American Cemetery and Memorial in Normandy

12

War Deaths—Folly Paid in Full

Tallies of worldwide war deaths vary widely, but it's in the order of sixty million souls or about 2.5 percent of the world's 1939 population. The Soviet Union paid the highest price, nearly twenty-four million dead, half of which were civilians. This incredible number represented about 13 percent of their population. Their next-door neighbor, Poland, had five million deaths, and these amounted to over 18 percent of their population, nearly all civilians. The little Baltic state of Lithuania had "only" half a million deaths, all civilians, and this represented 14 percent of their population.

China suffered nearly twenty million deaths, not quite 4 percent of their obviously very high population, of which 80 percent were civilians. The British and Americans had about the same death toll, approximately four hundred thousand, but in terms of percentage of population, Britain suffered twice that of the United States (0.8 percent vs. 0.4 percent).

Comparing the war deaths of the Axis powers with those of the Allies is also sobering. Axis deaths represented only 17 percent of all deaths in World War II, while the Allies shouldered the remaining 83 percent. The *military* deaths of the Axis were about half that of the Allies. It is also interesting to note that total deaths for Germany were about three times that for Japan (7.7 million vs. 2.5 million). Almost 11 percent of the German population was wiped out compared to about 6 percent for the Japanese. (Were we to have invaded the Japanese home islands, an additional five to ten million Japanese deaths were estimated, not to mention up to a million Allied deaths, mostly Americans).

Even more telling is the ratio of civilian to military deaths. The Axis civilians incurred just under 25 percent of total Axis deaths, while Allied civilians bore the brunt of the bloodbath, suffering 70 percent of total Allied deaths. In effect, the Allies suffered over fourteen times more civilian deaths than the Axis, largely endured by the Soviet Union and China. (In stark contrast, civilians comprised only 5 percent of all the deaths in World War I.)

This appalling waste of life, coupled with survivors' physical disabilities, mental trauma, broken homes, and lost education, plus the environmental damage and infrastructure destruction, have inestimable value. In addition to that priceless toll, the actual monetary expenditure for waging World War II has been put at nearly $20 trillion, at a time when the entire world's GNP was under $5 trillion (both in today's dollars).

Crop Duster

13

When Johnny Marched Home—The Wild Bunch?

Flying down our small town's main street, fifty feet above the ground in a Piper Cub, was a milk run for the ex-fighter pilot, but the hometown folks made it clear that this was a trifle reckless for their taste. Like many of our boys who grew up in a World War II combat venue, he had to adapt to new "Rules of Engagement" when it came to acceptable behavior. Out of admiration and sympathy, most civilians gave these returning combat vets a lot of slack, but they also expected them to eventually toe the line and integrate back into responsible peacetime behavior.

Returning veterans that had been in and around combat zones were exposed to carnage that often seriously damaged their psyche. But it seems the prevailing attitude was that combat fatigue was a temporary affliction and could be cured by the simple expediency of a short furlough away from combat.

However, a lingering combat fatigue in a few of our hometown vets was evident even to us amateurs. What we likely saw is now commonly referred to as post-traumatic stress disorder (PTSD). When such disorders eventually surfaced, most folks assumed a peacetime environment would provide the cure, as noted above.

This was possibly true for some, but we now know that many vets can greatly benefit from early professional help. As a case in point, we had an untreated shell-shocked World War I veteran in town who still exhibited occasional spells of aberrant behavior twenty-five years after the event.

Probably some vets were innately more boisterous than others. Our ex-Army Air Force fighter pilots appeared to be less domesticated than our bomber crews. The bomber crews I knew seemed inclined to marry the school sweetheart, find a local job, buy a home, and raise a family.

Two fighter pilots I knew became crop dusters, one of whom was killed while performing that service. Flying under power lines and barely clearing fences was standard operating procedure, and quickly dropping down over the field's tree line to get crops at the perimeter, then rapidly pulling up to miss the trees at the other end, was exciting to watch.

I'd sometimes have Pop drive me to the local airport to watch the boys come back in after an early morning of spraying. It was common to see remnants of pea vines or green bean vines dangling from an undercarriage—vines that don't grow more than a couple feet above the ground. Those boys loved flying and had the skill to circumvent the risk—most of the time.

World War II Canteen and Mess Kit

Swords to Plowshares—A Boy Scout Bonanza

The Herculean effort put forth by American industry during World War II built up huge inventories of war matériel that flooded the peacetime market following V-J Day. There were surplus fighting machines (airplanes, tanks, ships, etc.), arms (artillery, rifles, bombs, ammunition, etc.), and personnel supplies (clothing, helmets, K-rations, etc.). While the more dangerous equipment was scrapped or recycled, the government usually sold the other articles to the highest bidder for pennies on the dollar. A lively business of peddling low-cost war surplus items developed, with entrepreneurs amassing their own vast inventories for resale to the general public at still very low prices.

The Boy Scouts of America benefited from the treasure trove of low-cost surplus camping supplies. In my hometown, for example, we acquired backpacks, canteens, mess kits, pup tents, boots, blankets, raincoats, trenching shovels, nylon rope, and even the prepackaged preserved food. Many of us could not have otherwise afforded such gear simply for use as Boy Scout equipment.

Our troop also obtained South Pacific combat hammocks that featured a waterproof nylon roof, below which zippered mosquito netting extended all around down to the hammock itself. This was perfect for our overnight treks into the local woods. At campsites where trees were too far apart for hammocks, we had our two-man pup tents, which in our case were used by only one person. Compared to the hammocks, the tents were stuffier during hot summer nights. They also afforded less pest protection; although the entry had mosquito netting, there was no canvas floor, so bugs generally got in under the edges anyway. (Maybe the fallout from this resulted in the luxurious camping equipment you see today.)

Other camping aids, which we got cheap from GI survival kits, included compasses, knives, hatchets, waterproof matches, water-purifying tablets, and first-aid kits. All this stuff was brand-new, and we had to first learn how to wipe off the protective cosmoline coating on some of the metal objects before using them. (I recall that the surplus stores selling these goods literally reeked of cosmoline.)

There was another surplus component indispensable to our scouting experience: one of our Scout masters was a World War II combat vet. Apparently he had still more to give us boys than just the freedoms for which he'd recently risked his life to preserve.

Luftwaffe Me109

15

Working with the Enemy—The Lockheed Connection

The embryonic Ocean Systems Division of Lockheed Aircraft Company was staffed in large part by aeronautical engineers in the mid-1960s. Like many other large corporations, Lockheed was striving for a piece of the unprecedented government funding for developing undersea vehicles of all denominations. At only age thirty, my hiring on as an ex-employee of Electric Boat Company (makers of the world's finest combat submarines) put me in the advantageous position of being, by default, a relatively bona fide expert engineer in the underwater business.

Some of the aeronautical staff in Ocean Systems were immigrants, mostly from the Netherlands and Germany. I met a prominent executive in Ocean Systems I'll refer to as Willy, an ex-Luftwaffe test pilot, whose main claim to fame was surviving test flights of a manned version of the V-1 buzz-bomb. Teething problems with the V-1's guidance and stabilization systems prompted a conversion to a manned variant in the attempt to correct those issues.

By Willy's account, he and Hannah Reitsch, the famed German female test pilot, solved the problems. She and he lived to tell about it; several other pilots did not. The V-1's skimpy wings meant it glided like a brick. (Incidentally, another contemplated use of the manned version, the Fi 103R, was equivalent to the Japanese suicide kamikazes, but that idea was ultimately discarded on the basis of being "untraditional" for German warriors.)

Another ex-Luftwaffe pilot, whom I'll refer to as Harry, was assigned to me as a draftsman. He'd flown Me109s in the Italy campaign. According to one of our execs, who'd been a World War II NCO on a US destroyer off the Italian coast, he and Harry might have exchanged bullets. During a noontime conversation, Harry related that he'd been engaged in an offshore battle at the same time and place as had our exec.

The most revealing thing to me about Harry surfaced the first week he was assigned to my group. Being about fifteen years his junior, I got the distinct feeling during an informal conversation that he and another comrade in arms were sizing me up. He steered the discussion toward my nationality. After I divulged my ancestry as half Bohemian and half English, he turned to his buddy and said, "Close enough." I guess he saw my roots as being sufficiently Germanic to gain his tacit approval. Harry and I always had a very cordial working relationship so, at least in my case, maybe there was something to be said for his Hitlerjugend training.

EPILOGUE

Throughout the preceding essays, there is, for the sake of brevity, only passing reference to many interesting subjects and events with which you may be unfamiliar. For instance, many have never heard of the Niihau Incident mentioned in chapter 3. If your curiosity gets the better of you, which I truly hope it will, it's easy nowadays to delve into these areas through Internet research. By so doing, you'll discover a world of fascinating actions and outcomes that will supplement and probably modify your current understanding of World War II history.

World War II was largely a clash between militaristic, dictatorial governments and freedom-friendly, representative governments. In the 1930s, there was a growing belief of many people on both sides that dictatorships were the answer to our lingering, depression-laden world. It was evident that dictators could sidestep red tape and other governmental checks and balances that often stymied reforms needed for economic recovery. But we eventually saw that the corrupting influence of absolute power and the misjudgments of a single decision maker led to excesses and mistakes that culminated in national disaster. After the war, most would agree that there was some truth to the oft-quoted phrase "Democracy is the worst form of government, except for all the rest."

Another lesson learned was that without a strong military presence, a nation's diplomatic attempts to avert war with an aggressive foe are futile. The fallout from this was a colossal buildup of incredibly destructive weaponry, especially by the United States and the Soviet Union as the Cold War evolved after World War II. Adherents of this so-called Mutually Assured Destruction (MAD) strategy point to that policy as the reason another world war hasn't materialized over the past seventy years. Although some disarmament has occurred in recent decades, many nations still subsidize large, modern national-defense programs, relying on the premise that a strong *offense* is the best deterrent to attack. It would seem that being armed to the teeth and poised to rapidly inflict intolerable damage to one's antagonist is a key element in modern-day international politics.

ABOUT THE AUTHOR

William T. (Bill) Beran was at the impressionable age of almost seven years when the Pearl Harbor attack occurred. The visible anxiety and voiced concerns exhibited by his parents while they listened to radio accounts of that historic event struck a chord. His fascination with those exciting and deadly World War II years changed little over the following decades, yielding a lifelong interest in that period of history.

Beran hails from a small Wisconsin farming community, and his boyhood ambition during the war was to become a fighter pilot. This goal eventually faded as the war ended and eyesight shortcomings intervened. Instead, he obtained an engineering degree at the University of Wisconsin and, after two years active duty in the US Army, he embarked on a mechanical/marine engineering career, which was his passion and livelihood for over forty years. One outcome of that endeavor was his induction into the Offshore Energy Center's prestigious Technology Hall of Fame.

He and his wife, Luana, have been married for nearly fifty years and are blessed with four beautiful daughters and four delightful grandchildren. They are currently enjoying their retirement years in Montgomery, Texas.

LIST OF ILLUSTRATION CREDITS

Credit is given below for the illustrations preceding each chapter and also depicted in the cover's color collage:

Chapter 1   thinkstockphotos 92821817
Chapter 2   thinkstockphotos 114441463
Chapter 3   thinkstockphotos 492315936
Chapter 4   thinkstockphotos 498444645
Chapter 5   thinkstockphotos 100205006
Chapter 6   the author
Chapter 7   FDR Presidential Library & Museum
Chapter 8   thinkstockphotos SO001211
Chapter 9   US Army Center of Military History
             Publication 104-11
Chapter 10   thinkstockphotos 533341334
Chapter 11   the author
Chapter 12   thinkstockphotos 576914792
Chapter 13   thinkstockphotos 71263481
Chapter 14   thinkstockphotos 175442771
Chapter 15   Jim Larsen/Flying Heritage Museum

Printed in the United States
By Bookmasters